Scholastic Phonics

Crystals, Gems and Metals

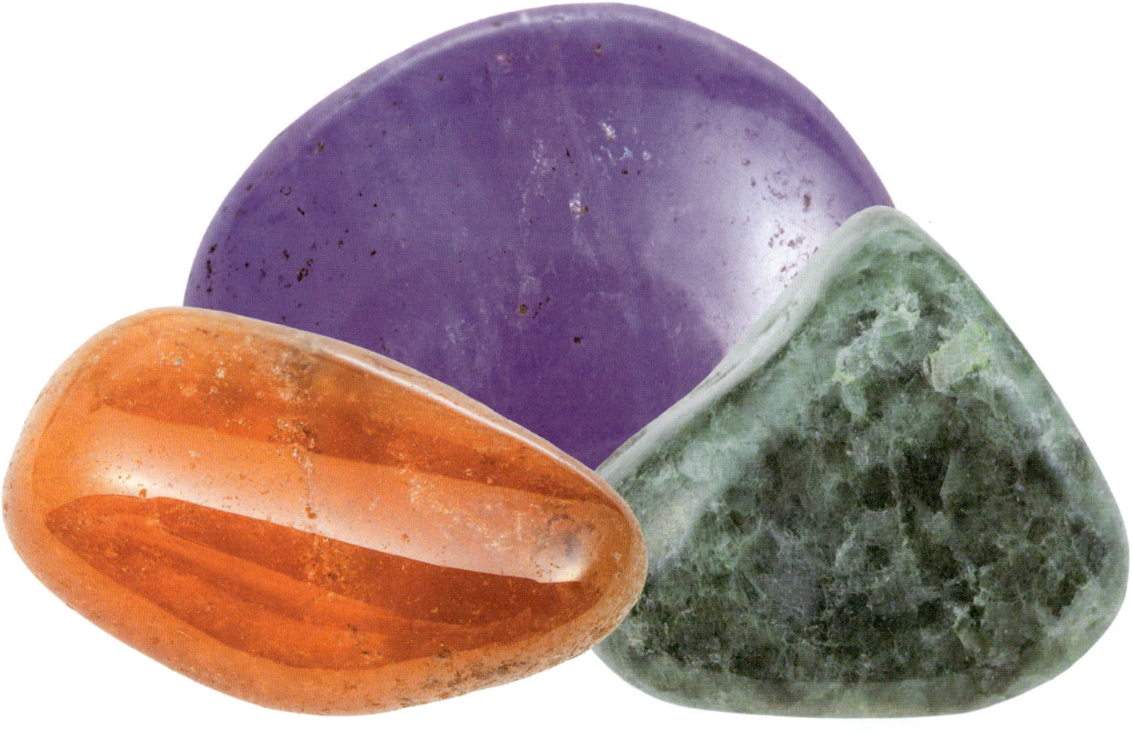

Published in the UK by Scholastic Education, 2023
Scholastic Distribution Centre, Bosworth Avenue, Tournament Fields, Warwick, CV34 6UQ
Scholastic Ireland, 89E Lagan Road, Dublin Industrial Estate, Glasnevin, Dublin, D11 HP5F

SCHOLASTIC and associated logos are trademarks and/or registered trademarks of Scholastic Inc.
www.scholastic.co.uk
© 2023 Scholastic
1 2 3 4 5 6 7 8 9   3 4 5 6 7 8 9 0 1 2

Printed by Ashford Colour Press
The book is made of materials from well-managed, FSC®-certified forests and other controlled sources.

A CIP catalogue record for this book is available from the British Library.
ISBN 978-0702-32119-1

All rights reserved. This book is sold subject to the condition that it shall not, by way of trade or otherwise, be lent, hired out or otherwise circulated in any form of binding or cover other than that in which it is published. No part of this publication may be reproduced, stored in a retrieval system, or transmitted in any form or by any other means (electronic, mechanical, photocopying, recording or otherwise) without prior written permission of Scholastic.

Every effort has been made to trace copyright holders for the works reproduced in this publication, and the publishers apologise for any inadvertent omissions.

Author
Giles Clare

Editorial team
Rachel Morgan, Vicki Yates, Gemma Smith, Jennie Clifford

Design team
Dipa Mistry, Andrea Lewis, We Are Grace

Illustrations
Eduardo Rubio Rincón/Advocate Art

Photographs
Cover stuartpitkin/iStock
p4 (gold collar) BOOCYS/Shutterstock, (crown) P Maxwell Photography/Shutterstock, (dagger hilt) Daniel Buxton UK/Shutterstock, (ring) JeweBewe/Shutterstock
p5 J. Palys/Shutterstock
p6 Byjeng/Shutterstock
p7 New Africa/Shutterstock
p8 Nancy_Zonneveld/Shutterstock
p9 (geode) Albert Russ/Shutterstock, (ring) Fruit_Cocktail/iStock
p10–11 Savany/iStock
p11 (inset) kakteen/Shutterstock
p12 JLco - Julia Amaral/iStock
p13 (diamond necklace) velveteye/iStock, (ruby cufflinks) Tarzhanova/Shutterstock, (emerald bracelet) Ins.C/Shutterstock, (tanzanite pendant) YolLusZam1802/Shutterstock
p14 (garnet, amethyst, peridot) vvoe/Shutterstock
p15 (moonstone, jade) vvoe/Shutterstock, (jasper) Sergey Dubrov/Shutterstock, (malachite) Nastya22/iStock
p16 volschenkh/iStock
p17 (pouring metal) Nordroden/iStock, (gold bars) VladKK/Shutterstock, (gold being bent) SviatlanaLaza/Shutterstock
p18 (coins) Eduardo Estellez/Shutterstock, (mask) Jaroslav Moravcik/Shutterstock, (knife) Leila Melhado/iStock
p19 (circuit board) Don Bendickson/Shutterstock, (boy) Gregory Johnston/Shutterstock
p20 Thais29/Shutterstock
p21 RuslanDashinsky/iStock
p21 (warning triangle) Fourleaflover/iStock

Help your child to read!

This book practises these letters and letter sounds.
Point and say the sounds with your child:

- ey (as in 'they')
- ere (as in 'here')
- su (as in 'usually')
- si (as in 'erosion')
- y (as in 'crystal')
- ti (as in 'condition')
- ssi (as in 'emissions')
- ci (as in 'special')
- our (as in 'pour')
- ore (as in 'more')

Your child may need help to read these common tricky words:

beautiful, people, pretty, are, because, the, of, into, to, many, once, today, our, were, anymore, two

Before reading
- Look at the cover picture and read the title together. Read the back cover blurb to your child.
- Ask your child: *Where do you find these things? What do people make with them?*
- Talk about the image in the magnifying glass.

During reading
- If your child gets stuck on a word, remind them to sound it out and then blend the sounds to read the word: p-r-o-f-e-ssi-o-n-al, professional.
- If they are still stuck, show them how to read the word.
- Enjoy looking at the pictures together. Pause to talk about the information.

After reading
- Talk about the images on page 24. What can your child tell you about them?
- Ask your child: *What are crystals and metal made from? How do you make gold into jewellery? Why do you think gemstones are expensive?*
- What was your favourite page in the book? Why?

Beautiful Objects

Since ancient times, people have made beautiful objects. Pretty gems and metals are called 'precious' because they are rare and expensive.

Minerals

Minerals are substances formed in the ground. The crystals here are pieces of minerals. Gold, silver and salt are also minerals.

Gemstones

Crystals can be shaped into beautiful gemstones. They are cut and polished by professionals, so light bounces off them. People adore how they sparkle.

Cut gemstones can be expensive! The professional here is assessing the condition of this gemstone. He will use it to make jewellery for a special occasion.

Rocks

Minerals are found in rocks. Crystals are usually easy to see. Metals are often mixed in with other minerals in rocks, called ores.

The purple crystal formation inside this rock is called amethyst.
Amethyst has been made into gemstones for many kings and queens.
Some people think it has healing powers.

Extraction

It is difficult to extract minerals from rocks. Miners work underground using drills and controlled explosions to break the rock. Even for professionals, it takes hard work and patience to find a few gemstones.

Some people think mining causes too much damage to nature. It can cause erosion (wear away the land) and can create harmful gas emissions.

Making Jewellery

Once cut and polished, gemstones are made into beautiful jewellery for special occasions. A jeweller uses a combination of gemstones and metals to make special designs.

Precious Gemstones

The jewellery here is made using four precious gemstones.

tanzanite

diamond

ruby

emerald

Semi-precious Gemstones

Some minerals are more common. They can be turned into pretty gemstones too, but they are not usually as valuable. These are called semi-precious, meaning half-precious.

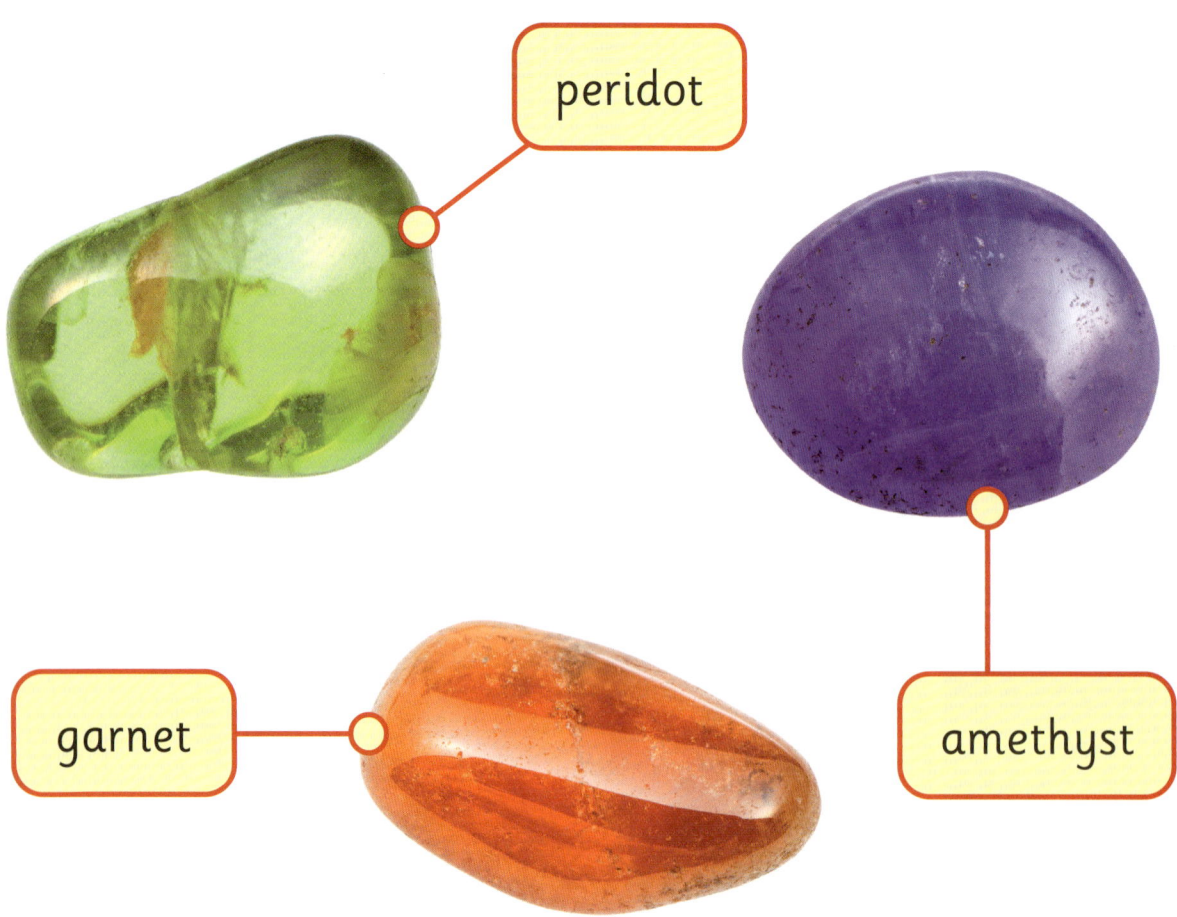

Precious Metals

Gold and silver are precious metals. Usually, the metal is hidden in rock, like tiny crumbs. Sometimes a seam of metal is visible in the rock – like the line of gold here.

gold

Melting Metals

Pieces of gold and silver can be melted down and poured into bar shapes. These metals can also be cut and bent.

Using Metals

People have been using gold to make special treasures for thousands of years.

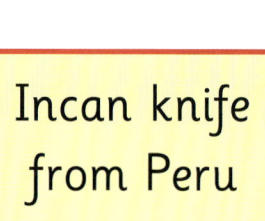

Incan knife from Peru

mask from ancient Egypt

coins from ancient Rome

Today, gold and silver are also used in other ways.

Silver in some T-shirts stops sweat smelling.

Gold helps the connections in our devices work better.

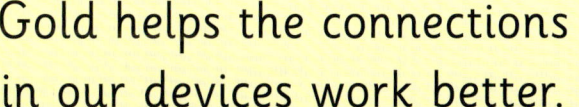

Salt Crystals

Salt is a mineral. In ancient times, it was expensive. People were sometimes paid in salt.

salt crystal formation

The Dead Sea in Jordan contains very salty water. Salt crystals make it easy to float. You can even read a newspaper here!

Grow Salt Crystals

⚠ Ask an adult to help you.

1. Pour hot water into a jar.

2. Pour table salt into the water.

3. Stir until the salt dissolves. Add more salt. Stir. Repeat until the salt won't dissolve anymore.

4. Hang string in the salty solution. Leave it still.

5. Wait two weeks for the crystals to grow.

Talk about it!